M000042050

AMERICAN HERITAGE

Rob & Angela Allison
scouter@allison.edu

 BOY SCOUTS OF AMERICA

Requirements

1. Read the Declaration of Independence. Pay close attention to the section that begins with "We hold these truths to be self-evident" and ends with "to provide new Guards for their future security." Rewrite that section in your own words, making it as easy to understand as possible. Then, share your writing with your merit badge counselor and discuss the importance of the Declaration to all Americans.

2. Do TWO of the following:

   a. Select two individuals from American history, one a political leader (a president, senator, etc.) and the other a private citizen (a writer, religious leader, etc.). Find out about each person's accomplishments and compare the contributions each has made to America's heritage.

   b. With your counselor's approval, choose an organization that has promoted some type of positive change in American society. Find out why the organization believed this change was necessary and how it helped to accomplish the change. Discuss how this organization is related to events or situations from America's past.

   c. With your counselor's approval, interview two veterans of the U.S. military. Find out what their experiences were like. Ask the veterans what they believe they accomplished.

   d. With your counselor's approval, interview three people in your community of different ages and occupations. Ask these people what America means to them, what they think is special about this country, and what American traditions they feel are important to preserve.

35852
ISBN 978-0-8395-3398-6
©2005 Boy Scouts of America
2010 Printing

BANG/Brainerd, MN
8-2010/060821

3. Do the following:

   a. Select a topic that is currently in the news. Describe to your counselor what is happening. Explain how today's events are related to or affected by the events and values of America's past.

   b. For each of the following, describe its adoption, tell about any changes since its adoption, and explain how each one continues to influence Americans today: the flag, the Pledge of Allegiance, the seal, the motto, and the national anthem.

   c. Research your family's history. Find out how various events and situations in American history affected your family. Share what you find with your counselor. Tell why your family came to America.

4. Do TWO of the following:

   a. Explain what is meant by the National Register of Historic Places. Describe how a property becomes eligible for listing. Make a map of your local area, marking the points of historical interest. Tell about any National Register properties in your area. Share the map with your counselor, and describe the historical points you have indicated.

   b. Research an event of historical importance that took place in or near your area. If possible, visit the place. Tell your counselor about the event and how it affected local history. Describe how the area looked then and what it now looks like.

   c. Find out when, why, and how your town or neighborhood started, and what ethnic, national, or racial groups played a part. Find out how the area has changed over the past 50 years and try to explain why.

   d. Take an active part in a program about an event or person in American history. Report to your counselor about the program, the part you took, and the subject.

   e. Visit a historic trail or walk in your area. After your visit, share with your counselor what you have learned. Discuss the importance of this location and explain why you think it might qualify for National Register listing.

5. Do ONE of the following:

   a. Watch two motion pictures (with the approval and permission of your counselor and parent) that are set in some period of American history. Describe to your counselor how accurate each film is with regard to the historical events depicted and also with regard to the way the characters are portrayed.

   b. Read a biography (with your counselor's approval) of someone who has made a contribution to America's heritage. Tell some things you admire about this individual and some things you do not admire. Explain why you think this person has made a positive or a negative contribution to America's heritage.

   c. Listen to recordings of popular songs from various periods of American history. Share five of these songs with your counselor, and describe how each song reflects the way people felt about the period in which it was popular. If a recording is not available, have a copy of the lyrics available.

6. Discuss with your counselor the career opportunities in American heritage. Pick one that interests you and explain how to prepare for this career. Discuss what education and training are required for this career.

Contents

Introduction

Think about this scenario: Your dad's college roommate was helping him study late one night at the dorm. They got hungry, but it was so late the pizza delivery was closed. So they had to drive to an all-night convenience store for snacks. On the way, they see one of your dad's classmates standing beside her stalled car. Your dad and his roommate offer to give her a ride home. They come inside to meet the girl's roommate—who, after a few years, becomes your mom.

Many events had to happen for your dad to meet your mom. That does not count all the events that had to happen for your dad's roommate to be there to help him study, for the girl's car to break down when and where it did, and for your future mom to be where she was at a certain moment in time.

If you think about it, history is sort of like that. Events of today are all connected to events of the past, whether the past is two hours ago or 200 years ago. You cannot have one without the other. Events that happened centuries ago, no matter how minor, probably affect what is happening today.

For instance, Michael Jordan may be one of the greatest basketball players of all time. He began his NBA career without controversy, but where would he be without the actions of people throughout history?

Go back about 200 years, when legal slavery in the South helped fuel the Civil War. When the war was settled, Reconstruction began with the intent of granting full civil rights to African Americans. Instead, Reconstruction angered many Southern whites, resulting in fierce racial discrimination in the South.

W. E. B. DuBois

Martin Luther King Jr.

Southern discrimination spurred African American activist W. E. B. DuBois to help create the National Association for the Advancement of Colored People in 1909. African American seamstress Rosa Parks joined the NAACP in 1943. When she was arrested in 1955 after refusing to give up her bus seat to a white man, the NAACP organized a local bus boycott. Local minister Martin Luther King Jr. transformed that boycott into a national movement for civil rights. And many years later, Michael Jordan, an African American athlete, enjoyed the fruits of that movement as he became known as one of the greatest basketball players of all time.

Of course, this example is very simple. In reality, thousands of events and millions of people worked together to shape the United States into a country where every person truly is equal. That is the heart of American heritage—people and events affecting one another over hundreds of years to get us where we are today. You must understand the events of yesterday to appreciate and understand the events of today. The past causes the present.

Understanding American heritage is not about memorizing historical dates and names. It is about understanding—for example, understanding current events that surround the signing of the Declaration of Independence, and why the signers believed this document was so vital to establishing the fundamental rights of the new republic. If you comprehend what the declaration meant to Americans then, you can appreciate how the past has influenced your present. Understanding your country's heritage is how you will come to truly know what it means to be an American.

Beginning at the Beginning

During the 1770s, American colonists were outraged. Although they had been loyal subjects to the crown of the British empire for years, Americans suddenly were feeling like second-class citizens.

To help raise money for a war with France, Britain had imposed taxes on everything from sugar to newspaper ads to paper to tea. While the colonists had paid taxes locally, this was the first time that the British Parliament—in which the colonists had no representation—was imposing taxes on the colonists alone. The colonists deserved to be treated with the same rights and privileges as the British citizens overseas. What was happening just was not fair.

Boston Tea Party

When a group of men from Boston, Massachusetts, dumped thousands of dollars worth of tea into the harbor in protest, the British responded harshly. They hurt local businesses by closing the Boston port, and they disbanded an elected council and outlawed town meetings. Americans wondered if what was happening in Boston could happen elsewhere in America.

Colonial leaders formed the first Continental Congress to address what they felt were unfair practices by Britain. Their goal was to put economic pressure on Britain—for instance, by boycotting British products—so that Britain would stop making harsh laws for the colonies. The Continental Congress drew up a list of complaints to send to Britain's King George III. There was little talk of independence; the colonists just wanted things returned to the way they had been.

King George III

King George never responded directly to the colonists' complaints. Instead, he declared a state of rebellion in the colonies in 1775 after colonists resisted the British attempt to destroy military stores at Lexington and Concord. By year's end, the king had banned all Colonial trade.

Still, American leaders like George Washington believed that they were fighting for their basic rights within the British Empire. It was a civil war, not a war for independence. But that feeling did not last. In June 1776, a committee was chosen to write "The Unanimous Declaration of the Thirteen United States of America." Today, we call this document the Declaration of Independence.

George Washington

The Declaration of Independence

As you read the declaration and put it into your own words, you will notice that it can be broken down into five basic parts.

The Introduction. This tells the reader that the declaration will explain the causes of America's need for independence from Great Britain.

The Preamble. This spells out the basic human rights to which the colonists believed everyone was entitled. It states that when people are denied these basic rights, it is their duty to overthrow and break free of whomever is denying them these rights.

The Body (first section). This is a list of "abuses" put forth by the king onto the colonists.

The Body (second section). This is a statement that the colonists had tried everything to solve these problems with Britain, without any luck.

The Conclusion. This states that because of these conditions, it is the colonists' right to separate from Britain. It declares the states free from the British empire. The 56 men who signed the Declaration of Independence knew full well that the penalty for it if they were caught by the British would be death.

When you read the Declaration of Independence, ask yourself the following questions:

- What rights did the colonists believe they had?

- Who gave them these rights, and who could take them away?

- What purpose did the government serve in securing these rights?

- Where did the government get its power?

The Declaration of Independence has inspired people in other countries to fight for basic rights, and it has inspired Americans to continue fighting for what they believe are the basic human rights entitled to them. As recently as 1963, Martin Luther King Jr. invoked the document as a way to show that all Americans—especially African Americans being discriminated against because of their race—deserve freedom. King stated: "I have a dream that one day this nation will rise up and live out the true meaning of its creed: 'We hold these truths to be self-evident: that all men are created equal.'"

Preamble to the Declaration of Independence

". . . We hold these truths to be self-evident, that all Men are created equal, that they are endowed by their Creator with certain unalienable Rights, that among these are Life, Liberty and the Pursuit of Happiness— That to secure these rights, Governments are instituted among Men, deriving their just powers from the consent of the governed—that whenever any Form of Government becomes destructive of these ends, it is the Right of the People to alter or to abolish it, and to institute new Government, laying its foundation on such principles and organizing its powers in such form, as to them shall seem most likely to effect their Safety and Happiness. Prudence, indeed, will dictate that Governments long established should not be changed for light and transient causes; and accordingly all experience hath shewn, that mankind are more disposed to suffer, while evils are sufferable, than to right themselves by abolishing the forms to which they are accustomed. But when a long train of abuses and usurpations, pursuing invariably the same Object evinces a design to reduce them under absolute Despotism, it is their right, it is their duty, to throw off such Government, and to provide new Guards for their future security. "

Symbolizing Independence

With the Declaration of Independence, the United States had inspiration to separate from Great Britain. To become an independent country, America needed its own symbols to establish an identity that was free and clear of Great Britain.

The symbols of the United States represent the country's core beliefs and values. They signify what it means to be an American. Many of these symbols have changed over the years, often to reflect the changing attitudes within the country. As you study America's symbols, it is important to think about what America's core values and beliefs mean to different Americans. What did those symbols mean to people when they were first adopted? What do they mean today?

The Stars and Stripes was Francis Scott Key's inspiration to write "The Star-Spangled Banner" in 1814.

The American Flag

The flag that flies in front of your school or your town hall is not the same one that colonists fought under during the American Revolution. In fact, the design of the United States flag has changed many times to reflect the changing country.

The first official U.S. flag was approved in 1777. To represent the 13 colonies, the flag had 13 horizontal stripes and 13 stars in the *canton,* or upper corner. There was no official design of the stars, so several patterns existed.

In 1795, two more stars and two more stripes were added to represent the newest states, Vermont and Kentucky. In 1818, after five more states had been admitted to the union, Congress decided that the flag would always have just 13 stripes, but the number of stars would reflect the number of states. The most recent change to the flag was in 1960, after Hawaii became a U.S. state. Someday you may see additional changes to the flag, for instance, if an American territory such as Puerto Rico is admitted into the union.

The U.S. flag is the ultimate symbol of this country's freedom. It inspired Francis Scott Key to write "The Star-Spangled Banner." The flag symbolizes freedom, not only for Americans, but for people around the world.

Pledge of Allegiance

"I pledge allegiance to my Flag and the Republic for which it stands; one nation indivisible, with liberty and justice for all." That was the original Pledge of Allegiance, as published in 1892.

In 1924, the phrase "my Flag" was replaced with "the flag of the United States of America." The pledge became official in 1942 but underwent one more change in 1954, when President Dwight D. Eisenhower added the phrase "under God." And there is always the possibility that the pledge could undergo more changes in the future.

Some people believe the phrase "under God" violates America's separation of church and state. In 2002, a man sued the government to take out the phrase. On Flag Day two years later, the Supreme Court dismissed the case. The ruling ensures that students will continue to be able to recite the pledge at school.

The Great Seal and Bald Eagle

Look on the back of a dollar bill, and you will see the front and back of the Great Seal of the United States. Adopted in 1782 after six years of designs and debates, the seal represents the country's core values and beliefs.

The original design called for an imperial eagle, but early Americans decided that the seal should be truly American. That is when the American bald eagle became the main element on the front of the seal. In one talon is a bundle of 13 arrows (representing the 13 colonies), in the other, an olive branch. The olive branch and arrows symbolize the power of both peace and war. In its mouth, the eagle holds an inscription: *E Pluribus Unum,* which is Latin for "out of many, one" and represents the union of the American people.

The Great Seal

The reverse side of the seal shows a 13-step, unfinished pyramid representing the original 13 colonies and showing that the country is always building and changing. The eye and the motto over it, *Annuit Coeptis* ("He has favored our undertakings"), allude to divine—or God's—intervention in the success of the country. The letters and numbers on the first step of the pyramid are Roman numerals for 1776, the year the Declaration of Independence was signed. The motto *Novus Ordo Seclorum,* "a new order of the ages," signifies a new era of American influence.

In God We Trust

Religion has always played a role in American heritage. Freedom of religion—allowing citizens to worship how they choose—is one of the core values upon which the United States was formed. The founding fathers believed that a supreme power had guided them in their fight for independence, so it is no surprise that references to God appear in the Declaration of Independence, the Constitution, and the national anthem.

"In God We Trust"

The thirteen-step pyramid on the Great Seal represents the 13 original colonies.

The phrase "In God We Trust" began appearing on American coins in 1864, during the Civil War. In 1908, legislation made it mandatory to include the motto on all coins issued in the United States, and in 1955 the motto was added to all paper money as well. In 1956, "In God We Trust" became our national motto.

The national motto has been challenged in court at least three times. Some people are concerned that the motto forces religion upon people. The courts usually have decided, however, that the motto is not a religious statement. It is more of a reflection of American heritage, in which religion has played a role.

The National Anthem

In 1814, America was at war with Britain once again. A lawyer named Francis Scott Key had boarded a British ship to try to free a friend and became trapped in the middle of the battle. From the ship, he watched as the British fired upon Fort McHenry in Baltimore, Maryland.

Then one night, the shelling stopped. Had the Americans surrendered? Had the British given up? As the sun began to rise, Key saw the American flag was still flying high over the fort. The United States had won the battle. Key was inspired to write a poem he called "Defence of Fort M'Henry," a title that later became "The Star-Spangled Banner."

Americans adopted "The Star-Spangled Banner" as their national anthem more than a century before Congress made it official in 1931.

Francis Scott Key

The Star-Spangled Banner

By Francis Scott Key, 1814

O say, can you see, by the dawn's early light,
What so proudly we hail'd at the twilight's last gleaming?
Whose broad stripes and bright stars, thro' the perilous fight,
O'er the ramparts we watch'd, were so gallantly streaming?
And the rockets' red glare, the bombs bursting in air,
Gave proof thro' the night that our flag was still there.
O say, does that star-spangled banner yet wave
O'er the land of the free and the home of the brave?

When dawn arose over the remains of a British-American naval battle, Francis Scott Key was inspired to write.

American bald eagle

Heritage at Home

To find out how to learn more about your own family heritage, see the resources section at the end of this pamphlet.

Americans are known around the world for their independent thinking and innovative ideas. They cherish their right to act and speak as they please—as long as it does not hurt anyone else. Americans know that with hard, honest work, the possibilities of what they can achieve are limitless.

These values have been associated with the United States since the country's beginning. In few other countries do all people enjoy such freedom, and that makes people proud to be Americans and willing to defend their country and its values.

Family and Freedom

No matter if your family came over on the *Mayflower* or if you are the first person in your family to be born in the United States, your family history is important. Understanding how your family came to the United States and what experiences they had can help you understand American heritage.

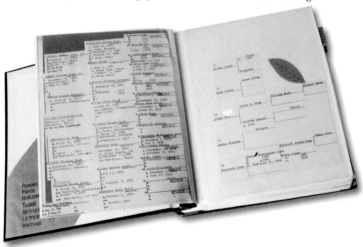

Immigrants arriving at Ellis Island

Only a few Americans can trace their families back to the native people who were here before Europeans landed. Most families arrived here to try to increase their fortunes or to escape a hard life, as many Asian and European immigrants did in the 1800s. Or they could have arrived after a forced journey as an African slave.

Learning why your family came to America and how they took part in American history—whether it was fighting in the Civil War, helping to build a railroad that would connect opposite ends of the country, marching in a protest for equal rights for women, or simply casting their vote for a president—helps you understand why history is more than just dates and names. It is real people living real lives, whose actions—no matter how small—affect the future.

Start researching your family history by talking to your parents. Find out when and where they were born, where they grew up, and how they met. Ask them what major events affected their lives and how they responded to them. See if they have any documents for you to look at, such as birth and death certificates or a family Bible with names and dates in it.

Americans' right to vote as their hearts lead them is a basic part of our freedom.

For more information about researching your family's history, read the *Genealogy* merit badge pamphlet. The resources listed at the end of this pamphlet will give you some information, too.

Researching your family history goes beyond learning about American heritage. Knowing about your family's role in the history of this country can teach you about what American ideals and traditions are important to your family—things that you can proudly pass down to your own children.

Ask other relatives—especially older ones—the same questions. Talk to your grandparents about where they came from, and find out if they have any living relatives you can interview as well. Ask them for stories about their lives growing up as well as what *their* parents and grandparents were like. Where did they grow up? What did they do for a living? How did they participate in the major events of the times? What family traditions did they have? Make sure to record your interviews so you do not forget anything.

Ask your relatives to show you some old family photographs and tell you what they remember about the lives of the relatives pictured.

Family Research Resources

There are many genealogical societies and organizations that can help you in your search. The Church of Jesus Christ of Latter-day Saints operates the Family History Library and more than 4,000 branch libraries called Family History Centers. Their files contain millions of family names. You can see what kinds of records they have online, and volunteers at the centers can help you find the information you are looking for—just do not ask them to do the research for you.

The American Family Immigration History Center provides information about the 22 million passengers and ships' crews who passed through New York City's Ellis Island between 1892 and 1924. For instance, if you think your great-great-grandmother arrived from Europe sometime around 1901, chances are that her passenger record is on file. Plugging in her name at the center's Web site may call up her date of arrival, how old she was, what town and country she came from, her port of departure, and her marital status.

Defending Freedom

America's heritage also has been molded by its citizens in defense of the liberties they hold dear. Of course, the people most directly linked to this phase of American heritage are those who have defended it in conflicts both near and abroad—our military.

Local Veterans Affairs offices or Veterans of Foreign Wars posts can recommend a veteran whom you could interview. See the resources section at the end of this pamphlet for more information.

Talking to military veterans is a great way to learn about what being an American means to its citizens. You probably know someone—or know someone who knows someone—who has served or is serving in the military. These veterans and active soldiers usually are happy to talk about their experiences defending the country and its values, whether in wartime or peacetime.

Everyday People

Nonmilitary citizens also have strong feelings about what it means to be an American. Their views can differ depending on their ages. Consider what effect growing up in different time periods will have on citizens. For example, think about how growing up during one of the following periods of history would have affected you.

Some people lost their homes during the 1930s and lived in roadside communities that sprang up on the outskirts of many large cities.

The Great Depression (1929–1939)

When stock market prices plummeted in 1929, many people were financially ruined. By 1932, about 30 percent of the workforce was unemployed, and by 1933, almost half of U.S. banks had failed. Americans learned to be extremely frugal, saving money as best they could. Many kept their money in their homes instead of in banks, and many depended heavily on government programs for help.

World War II (1941–1945)

When Japanese forces attacked Hawaii's Pearl Harbor on December 7, 1941, Americans rallied to defend their country. America immediately entered World War II, and the U.S. Army quickly expanded from about 1.6 million soldiers to about 8.3 million. Civilians who traditionally were not part of the workforce—mostly women and African Americans—took positions in factories to help support the troops.

Although most of America was united in the war, other groups were not allowed to participate. For instance, under what was called national security, many Japanese Americans were rounded up and held in internment camps. They were basically prisoners because of their Japanese descent. In recent years, the U.S. government has made reparations to many of the Japanese American families who suffered losses during that time.

Advertising campaigns featuring Rosie the Riveter encouraged women to join the workforce during World War II.

Martin Luther King Jr. called for nonviolent demonstrations in the fight for civil rights.

The Civil Rights Movement (1950s and 1960s)

The civil rights crisis divided the country like no other issue since the Civil War. In the southern states, African Americans were not allowed to attend school or eat in restaurants with whites—even their drinking fountains and rest rooms were separate. Blacks had more freedom in the northern states, but discrimination still was evident in things like employment and housing. Civil rights demonstrations often turned violent. Riots sometimes broke out as leaders on both sides tried to defend their beliefs. It was not until the Civil Rights Act of 1964 and the Voting Rights Act of 1965 that serious progress was made toward equal treatment of the races.

The Korean War (1950–1953)

This war placed many Americans at the forefront of the battle against Communism, as North Korea invaded South Korea. While America's presence in the war was short-lived, it was among the deadliest for American soldiers.

Boom in California (1950s–1960s)

America's population boomed after World War II, and California was perhaps affected most. Its cities exploded with new housing and highways, and many icons of American culture migrated from New York to Los Angeles. Among the most notable arrivals to the new West Coast scene were television production studios and Brooklyn's beloved baseball team, the Dodgers.

The Space Race

Until 1957, when the Russians launched Sputnik I, the first space satellite, Americans relied on jet test pilots to reach new frontiers in flight. Their spirits soared with hope after President John F. Kennedy's optimistic promise to land on the moon by the end of the 1960s. His vision was reached in July 1969, when Apollo 11 astronauts successfully landed on the moon and returned to Earth.

Astronaut Neil Armstrong, the first man to step on the moon, was an Eagle Scout.

Technological Boom

In the '50s, '60s, and '70s, Americans were treated to technological advances that were designed for more convenience in their homes. From TV dinners to live television via satellite, advancements resulted in more convenience and immediacy for the average American.

The 1970s

Americans' morale seemed to dip during this decade because of several events. The Vietnam War grew unpopular as more and more Americans began to question why we were fighting. The Watergate scandal forced President Richard Nixon to resign after he was accused of covering up a break-in at his rival's headquarters. The country also plunged into a deep recession, in which prices were high and an oil shortage forced cars to line up for hours at gas stations.

Interviewing Tips

If you choose either option 2c or 2d, here are some basic tips to remember as you plan your interviews.

- When coming up with questions to ask people, start with the *five Ws and H* that journalists use to get their story: *who, what, when, where, why, and how.* Questions that start with those words will help stir the memory of the person you are interviewing, and they will help you think of other interesting questions.

- Ask easy questions first, such as the person's name, age, and where they live. This helps them become comfortable as you proceed to more difficult, thought-provoking questions.

- Form your questions so that the person you are interviewing must answer with more than "yes" or "no." An example of such a question might be "Tell me why you enjoyed your service in the Navy" instead of "Did you like your service in the Navy?"

- Ask follow-up questions like "Can you be more specific?" and "Can you give me an example?"

- Record the interview. (Make sure to get permission from your interview subject first.) Most people talk too fast for you to write down complete answers, and taping an interview will make sure you do not miss a thing.

The Vietnam Veterans Memorial in Washington, D.C.

Power of the People

Not all history makers need to be George Washington or Martin Luther King Jr. While these men certainly left their fingerprints on American history, many ordinary citizens have made lasting impressions as well.

From Ordinary to Extraordinary

Our 39th president, Jimmy Carter, may be about the most shining example of "ordinary to extraordinary." He was born in 1924 and grew up in rural Georgia. Carter was educated in the public school system and later attended Georgia Southwestern College, the Georgia Institute of Technology, and the U.S. Naval Academy. He also did graduate work in nuclear physics at Union College in New York.

His father was a farmer and business owner; his mother, a nurse. In 1953, after his father's death, Jimmy Carter resigned from his commission with the U.S. Navy to take care of the family business. His interest in education eventually led him to politics. Carter served as U.S. president from 1977 to 1981. During that time, his administration focused on foreign relations, human rights, and environmental issues.

Since leaving office, Carter has continued his service to the public and to those who are less fortunate. He teaches Sunday school and does volunteer work for many organizations, among them Habitat for Humanity.

Lawyer Francis Scott Key probably had no idea that his poem would someday become America's national anthem. Independence, freedom, and innovativeness are all associated with the United States, and even the most "average" American citizens have become known for working to further the ideals of their country.

The President and the Preacher

Learning about how public and private citizens have changed history can be as easy as going to the library. Decide what time period you are interested in, or ask the librarian for a recommendation, and then head over to the library's biography section.

If you choose option 2a, you might consider comparing two figures from similar times in history, such as President John F. Kennedy and Martin Luther King Jr. Both men worked to promote the values of the United States, but each had a unique approach.

John F. Kennedy

The grandson of a Boston mayor, John Fitzgerald Kennedy had a heritage of public service. Kennedy planned on becoming a teacher or a writer after his service in World War II, but when his politically ambitious brother Joe was killed, John Kennedy changed his career plans.

Kennedy served three terms in the U.S. House of Representatives and was later elected to the U.S. Senate. He professed to represent the values of regular Americans and pushed for better working conditions, more public housing, higher wages, and lower prices.

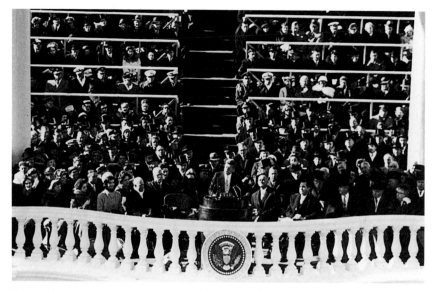

In his inaugural speech in January 1961, President Kennedy implored Americans: "Ask not what your country can do for you—ask what you can do for your country."

Kennedy understood the power of the people. On the eve of the 1960 presidential election, he helped release Martin Luther King Jr. from prison. The resulting support from African Americans may have helped Kennedy become the youngest American president.

As president, Kennedy championed many causes he felt would strengthen America, including the Peace Corps and the space program. He supported the civil rights movement, believing that it was important to show the world that the best way to live was in a free and democratic society such as America. Yet during this time, African Americans were not really free.

Kennedy was worried that activists' protests and demonstrations would anger white people and create resistance toward civil rights legislation. After many Americans viewed a violent protest on television news, Kennedy addressed the nation about the civil rights crisis. "This nation was founded by men of many nations and backgrounds," he said. "It was founded on the principle that all men are created equal, and that the rights of every man are diminished when the rights of one man are threatened."

Soon after, Kennedy started gathering support from both Democrats and Republicans for a civil rights program. The proposed legislation was making rounds through Congress when Kennedy was assassinated on November 22, 1963. It would be up to his replacement, Lyndon Baines Johnson, to usher the civil rights bill into law.

Martin Luther King Jr.

Growing up in the South, Martin Luther King Jr. thought the separation of races was normal. As a young adult, he visited Connecticut, where he saw blacks and whites eating together and attending the same church. This was how America was supposed to be, he thought.

King studied law and medicine in college but ultimately decided to follow in his father's footsteps, entering public service through the ministry. An eloquent speaker, King could help his church members spiritually, but he also could inspire them to demand equality.

Rosa Parks' refusal to give up her bus seat to a white man helped spark the beginning of the civil rights movement.

King's first test came in 1955, when he was chosen to lead bus boycotts in Montgomery, Alabama, after Rosa Parks refused to give up her seat to a white man. King was only 26 years old, but he inspired African Americans to stop riding on buses until the city's buses were desegregated a year later.

Realizing the power that ordinary people could have over discrimination, King began working toward a mass movement for civil rights. Forming the Southern Christian Leadership Conference, he began speaking all over the country. He called for nonviolent protests. Although he encouraged legal action from the government, he did not feel like the government was doing enough. "Nonviolence can touch men where the law cannot reach them," he said.

King's work was dangerous. He was arrested many times. His house and church were bombed. One time he was even stabbed. But he believed that his sacrifices were necessary to show how much he believed in what America could be.

During the March on Washington in 1963, Martin Luther King Jr. delivered his famous "I have a dream" speech, saying, "I have a dream that my four children will one day live in a nation where they will not be judged by the color of their skin but by the content of their character."

In perhaps the most wide-reaching demonstration, King and other civil rights leaders organized the March on Washington. On August 28, 1963, Americans watched on TV as more than 200,000 people—both blacks and whites—peacefully come together to demand equal rights for all races. Soon most of the country supported a strong civil rights law, and the Civil Rights Act of 1964 was passed. The Voting Rights Act was passed a year later.

In 1968, King was assassinated in Tennessee. However, the civil rights movement has continued.

King and Kennedy both answered a call to service: Kennedy in the military and politics, King in the ministry. They both were powerful speakers and knew how to use the medium of television to their advantage. Both men had definite ideas of how America should be. In a sense, it was the same America, one where everyone had equal opportunities to succeed and be free. But they had different ways of achieving their goals. Kennedy wanted to use the law. King wanted to mobilize the people. Both methods worked. In fact, both methods probably were necessary to achieve the ultimate goal of racial equality.

Join Up

The actions of many people working toward a common goal can make a huge difference. Millions of Americans helped the Civil Rights Act of 1964 come to fruition. Each individual contributed in some way.

That is why people often join organizations. They have an issue that is important to them. They want to work with other people who feel the same way so that they can make a difference in American society. They may work to help a local political candidate get elected. They may volunteer to teach children to read. They may help organize marathons to raise money for disease research. Or they may write letters to government leaders to urge them to vote a certain way.

Ordinary People Who Made a Difference

Clara Barton (1821–1912). "Angel of the Civil War battlefield" and founder of the American Red Cross.

César Chávez (1927–1993). Helped organize a union of Hispanic and Filipino farm workers in 1962.

Frederick Douglass (1817–1895). Born a slave and became the first black man to stand boldly against slavery in America.

Bob Hope (1903–2003). Comedian and actor who entertained several generations, including U.S. soldiers overseas in service to their country.

Frederick Douglass

Barbara Jordan (1936–1996). Powerful orator and the first African American woman elected to the Texas Senate (1966) and U.S. House of Representatives (1972).

Helen Keller (1880–1968). Education reformer, lecturer, and writer who lost her sight and hearing at age 19 months.

Thurgood Marshall (1908–1993). The first African American justice to sit on the U.S. Supreme Court.

Thomas Paine (1737–1809). English-born philosopher whose pamphlet *Common Sense* argued for complete American independence from Britain.

Sally K. Ride (1951–). The first American woman in space, as a crewmember of the space shuttle *Challenger* in 1983.

Jackie Robinson (1919–1972). African American baseball player whose athletic prowess and determination helped break the color barrier in major-league sports.

Sam Walton (1918–1992). Businessman and entrepreneur whose centralized distribution system allowed his stores to buy high volumes of brand-name goods and sell them at discount prices.

Tiger Woods (1975–). Multiracial professional golfer whose exceptional play has made him the youngest player ever to reach such heights in the sport.

Thomas Paine

Jackie Robinson

It sometimes is hard to see how one person can make a difference. But one person working with other people toward a common cause can truly lead to changes. One example is the National Audubon Society. Because of the efforts of thousands of people, American wildlife has a better chance of survival.

In 1886, George Grinnell, the editor of *Forest and Stream* magazine, asked his readers to sign a pledge promising not to hurt birds. When about 40,000 people agreed, the Audubon Society for the Protection of Birds was founded. Membership grew so quickly that Grinnell was unable to keep pace with the growth. Ten years later, the Massachusetts Audubon Society was started when cousins Harriet Hemenway and Mirna Hall urged people to stop wearing feathered hats in order to halt the killing of birds. Soon people in more and more states were forming organizations under the name of the Audubon Society.

By 1901, a national organization, the National Committee of Audubon Societies—now known as the National Audubon Society—was born, with the purpose of protecting native birds and other wildlife. Members believe that the United States always has had a special relationship with its land. They believe that protecting and conserving the land and the creatures that live on it helps preserve our American heritage.

In 1901, the Florida Audubon Society discovered a colony of brown pelicans—the last of their kind—on the east coast of Florida. The society began a campaign to protect the pelicans. Two years later, President Theodore Roosevelt named Pelican Island as the first National Wildlife Refuge.

Your Friendly, Neighborhood Heritage

Let's say you live in Stillwater, Oklahoma, the home of Oklahoma State University. Researching the town's history will show you that the town started during the 1889 Oklahoma land rush, in which the government opened up Indian Territory to white settlers. The new settlement stood between two creeks but was miles from any railroad, which could bring in supplies and people, so the settlers lobbied for a new land-grant college to help increase the area's importance. In 1890, Oklahoma A&M College (now OSU) was founded. Without the college, the town of Stillwater might have disappeared—and you would be living somewhere else.

Learning about your town's history can bring American heritage alive by showing you how your life today has been affected by the past. Important questions can come up as you research your town's history. For instance, in the Stillwater example, you may wonder what industry developed in the town to make it successful, what happened to the American Indians who were displaced when white settlers rushed in, or whether African Americans, who were no longer slaves but often not granted the same rights as whites, were allowed to claim land. Finding the answers to thoughts like these will help you understand what your town was like when it began—and who contributed to its history.

Town Secrets

Your local library is a great place to find information about your town's history. The library can provide you with books written by local historians or files of other historical resources.

Knowing how the Dust Bowl era might have affected your town is part of understanding its history.

Most libraries also have archives of the local newspaper on microfilm that often date back to the town's founding. These old newspapers can introduce the town's founders and the circumstances around the town's beginning, and they can describe historical events that affected the town.

For instance, the Great Depression of the 1930s affected the entire country but particularly farmers. In Oklahoma, the Dust Bowl ruined many crops and forced farmers westward toward California. This phenomenal disaster lasted about a decade and helped lengthen the Depression and its devastating effects. Reading accounts of those hard times can help you research how the Dust Bowl might have affected your town.

To begin your historical research, visit your local museum or library.

State and local historical societies can help you uncover more local history, and most towns also have a city museum dedicated to preserving the heritage of the place where you live. Plugging the state historical society's name into your Web

Internet research is fast and fun, but be sure you have your parent's permission first.

browser might lead you to a list of historical sites in your area. These sites also can tell you if your city or county has its own historical society.

Census records have lots of statistics about the people in your town. These records can give you current numbers for population, sex, race, age, and many other facts. Start your research by visiting the Web site of the U.S. Census Bureau. (See the resources section for more information.)

Census records for past statistics are often archived at your local library. You can check with your federal depository library, too. The Federal Depository Library Program collects information from all three branches of the government and distributes it to the public for free. Almost every congressional district has one. You can visit the program's Web site to find all the libraries in your state that have been designated as federal depositories. (See the resources section for more information.) There should be one near you, but call first to make sure the library has the information you are seeking.

Registered History

When you think of San Francisco, California, what comes to mind? You might think of the infamous Alcatraz Island, where the country's most notorious criminals were once held. There is a good chance you would think of the cable cars that—without engines—amazingly maneuver the city's hills. But you probably would not take particular notice of the Bank of Italy on Montgomery Street. Started by the son of Italian immigrants in 1904, the bank helped to rebuild San Francisco after the Great Earthquake of 1906. Today, you might know it as Bank of America.

Alcatraz Island

A San Francisco cable car

These sites are important to our American heritage, and they are listed on the National Register of Historic Places. Authorized under the National Historic Preservation Act of 1966, the register coordinates and supports efforts to identify, evaluate, and protect historic and archaeological resources.

The National Register does not list all historic properties. There are very specific criteria for a property to be listed. Above all, the property must be significant in American history, architecture, archaeology, and culture. The property also must be one of the following.

- It must be associated with events that have contributed significantly to American heritage.

- It must be associated with important people in American heritage.

- It must represent characteristics of a type, period, or method of construction; be the work of a respected artist; or have artistic value.

- It must have the potential to result in important historical (or prehistorical) information.

Generally, birthplaces and grave sites of famous people, as well as properties that are less than 50 years old, are not eligible unless they are architecturally valuable or no other appropriate site can be associated with that person.

Mapping It Out. Once you have found what National Register properties are in your area, plot them on a map. Your map does not have to be exact, but it should identify major streets, highways, and natural resources such as lakes and rivers. Your local library, Chamber of Commerce, or realty office might be able to provide you with a map of your town. Your city's Web site also may have a link to a map you can print out; just plug in the town and state name in your browser to begin the search.

With more than 77,000 listings, there is a good chance a property in your town is listed on the National Register. You can enter your town's name (or your county's name, if you live in a small town) on the National Register's Web site to find out what properties are there. See the resources section at the end of this pamphlet.

Take a Hike

One way to explore all this history yourself is to take a hike on a historic trail near where you live. For a list of historic trails approved by the Boy Scouts of America, go to *http://www.scouting.org/boyscouts/trails.* Select your state and the trail rating. You will then be linked to a listing of all the trails in your state.

Celebrating History

Most towns and cities have plenty of events to celebrate history. By participating in those events, you can learn why these events are significant. (You probably will have fun doing them, too.) Look for events surrounding local heritage, such as Mardi Gras in New Orleans or the return of the swallows to Capistrano, California.

Many towns sponsor fireworks shows to celebrate the 4th of July.

Some festivities are celebrated regionally. For instance, many African Americans celebrate Juneteenth (June 19), the day in 1865 when slaves in Galveston, Texas, learned that the Civil War was over.

Many towns and cities celebrate local historical events and people. There may be a battlefield in your area that allows people to participate in reenactments. Public ceremonies often are held at famous grave sites, such as George Washington's burial place at Mount Vernon, Virginia. Smaller towns might have a Founders Day celebration, where parades and festivals mark the anniversary of the town's beginning. Some states celebrate an Admissions Day, the day that the state was admitted into the union.

Check out your town's community calendar for listings of events. Many organizations—such as the library, chamber of commerce, newspaper, or city hall—let people add their events to the calendar. You also can plug in your town's name and the words "community calendar" into an Internet search engine. Talk with officials from your local city museum or historical society to see if they can suggest upcoming events, such as plays or shows about local history produced by your local theater group.

George Washington's tomb at Mount Vernon, Virginia

History Like You Have Never Seen—or Heard

Ever since 1891, when Thomas Edison received a patent for his motion-picture camera, the United States has been a leader in the motion-picture industry. Movies can reflect who we are as a country. They can show the best of America, and they can show the worst of America. They can tell stories about real events, and they can show what life was like during a certain time period.

Thomas Edison

Movies that deal with history should be watched carefully. Directors sometimes have a certain point of view they want to get across to their audience. They may portray characters and events negatively or positively so that the audience feels a certain way about the subject.

For instance, many American Indians were portrayed as villains in "spaghetti" Westerns—popular, low-budget films of the 1960s that were financed by Italian companies. This may have been because of prejudice on the part of moviemakers, or simply to show the white characters as more heroic.

Other historical movies may add information that never really happened. Often this is to make the movie more exciting (at least, according to the director). A historical movie sometimes can sway the audience simply because of what it leaves out. It is up to you to research and find out what actually happened.

It's not possible to fit the whole story into a movie. If you want to know the full story, you may want to do some additional research and reading.

History on Film

Period	Title (Rating)	Year
American Revolution/ Colonial Times	*1776* (G)	1972
Civil War	*Buffalo Soldiers* (PG)	1997
	Gettysburg (PG)	1993
	The Red Badge of Courage (NR)	1951
	Gone With the Wind (G)	1939
The Old West	*Dances With Wolves* (PG-13)	1990
	Lonesome Dove (NR)	1989
	Gunfight at the O.K. Corral (NR)	1957
World War I	*A Farewell to Arms* (NR)	1957
	Sergeant York (NR)	1941
	All Quiet on the Western Front (NR)	1930
The Great Depression	*The Journey of Natty Gann* (PG)	1985
	Sounder (G)	1972
	To Kill a Mockingbird (NR)	1962
	The Grapes of Wrath (NR)	1940
World War II	*Band of Brothers* (NR)	2001
	The Tuskegee Airmen (PG-13)	1995
	Memphis Belle (PG-13)	1990
	Tora! Tora! Tora! (G)	1970
	The Longest Day (NR)	1962
	Sands of Iwo Jima (NR)	1949
	The Best Years of Our Lives (NR)	1946
The 1950s	*La Bamba* (PG-13)	1987
	Grease (PG)	1978
	Rebel Without a Cause (NR)	1955
The Space Race	*Apollo 13* (PG)	1995
	The Right Stuff (PG)	1983
Civil Rights and Tolerance	*Ghosts of Mississippi* (PG-13)	1996
	Corrina, Corrina (PG)	1994
	The Long Walk Home (PG-13)	1990
	Driving Miss Daisy (PG)	1989
	King (NR)	1978
	The Autobiography of Miss Jane Pittman (NR)	1974

Mark Carnes, the editor of *Past Imperfect: History According to the Movies,* probably gives the best advice about learning history from film. In a television interview, he said, "What I should do whenever I go to a movie, or whenever anyone goes to a movie, is enjoy it . . . and not believe a word." And then, he advises, read about the history.

Listen Up

What are you listening to right now? Is it the hot new single on the radio? Your parent's favorite golden oldie? Or your little sister or brother's kid tunes? No matter what you are listening to, someone is probably trying to tell you something.

That is the way American music has been since the first settlers set foot on American soil. Music today is a lot like music of yesterday. Songs are basically about emotion. Singers express feelings of love, spirituality, patriotism, and life in general.

It is not always possible to fully understand the meaning of a song unless you personally ask the songwriter—and most of the time that is impossible. And songs are often open to many different interpretations. But if you read the lyrics closely, there are ways you can make certain assumptions.

- Find out when the song was written. Was there an important event going on at the time that may have influenced the song? What was the mood of the country like at the time? Were people patriotic in a time of war, or were they rebellious in a time of protest?

- Find out who wrote the song. What was the author's ethnic background? Male or female? Young or old? How would what was going on in the country at the time the song was written affect the writer?

- Was the song written with someone in mind? Is there a particular audience the songwriter intended to reach? Is the songwriter sharing similar thoughts and feelings, or trying to convince others who may disagree with him that his view is the correct one?

- What words or phrases are repeated? Often these *hooks* are important to the writer and may have special meaning.

- Why was the song written? Was it to remind Americans to value their freedom? Was it to express pride in the strength of the nation?

- How would people with different backgrounds interpret the song?

Many CDs include the written lyrics of popular songs. You may own the CD, or your public library may have it available. Often these lyrics are online as well. Just plug in the name of the song and the word "lyrics" into your Web browser. Music stores can be another good source of sheet music with lyrics. Your local library may have songbooks and sheet music on file.

Older song lyrics can be found online. The Web addresses of some collection sites are included in the resources section. Be sure you have your parent's permission whenever you go online.

Songs of the Times

Colonial Times (mid- to late 1700s). Most people sang hymns, but as independence loomed, American songwriters began comparing biblical struggles with struggles against Britain. Songs also told about current events—such as a new settlement or a battle victory. "The Liberty Song," written by Revolutionary War hero John Dickinson, was a song of the times.

Slavery. Many songs sung by slaves helped them keep rhythm while they were working. The songs often were about brutality and injustice, but no one but the slaves could tell. Often they were singing in front of their masters, so they had to hide the true meaning of their words. For example, "Go Down, Moses" recalls a story from the Christian Bible about the Hebrews held in bondage in Egypt.

Pre–Civil War (early to mid-1800s). Songs about social reform became popular and warned people about the dangers of drinking and the immorality of slavery. "Buffalo Gals," written by John Hodges and John Lomax, was popular in minstrel shows.

Civil War (1861–1865). Songs fueled patriotism on both sides of the battle. The songs tried to show why one side deserved to win or expressed vengeance against the enemy. "The Battle Hymn of the Republic" is a song from that era that is still sung today.

Post–Civil War (late 1800s). Songs often reflected America's westward movement. Cowboys, miners, loggers, and homesteaders—both the white settlers and the Spanish people already there—were popular themes. "I've Been Working on the Railroad" and "Clementine" are tunes you might recognize.

Early 20th Century. One style of music reflected the consciousness of the new arrivals to America. As immigrants flooded into America, citizens struggled to find a national identity, so patriotic songs once again became popular. Another style of the era came from African Americans, who were no longer slaves but still faced discrimination and continued to sing about hardships. This style of music was called the *blues*. Still other styles of music in the early 20th century, such as ragtime and jazz, reflected the prosperity and lifestyles of the time.

The Great Depression (1929 through early 1930s). United in poverty and hardship, people in this era wrote songs that reflected the shared experiences of life during the Depression. The title of "Dust Bowl Blues" sums up the music of the era.

World War II. Patriotic songs again were on the rise, as well as songs that reflected American values to keep up people's spirits while soldiers were overseas. The swinging tune of "Boogie Woogie Bugle Boy" kept toes tapping on all fronts.

1950s. A new breed of Americans was on the rise: the teenager. Teens struggled to find their own identity, separate from their parents, without the restrictions of an earlier age. The result? Rebellious rock and roll.

Teens in the 1950s at the hop

Vietnam War. The generation gap between young and old grew even wider as the war continued. In protest, many songs lashed out against adult authority.

1970s. The aftershock of the 1960s produced songs that echoed cultural awareness in the early 1970s. As profits replaced the message as the focal point of popular music, songs no longer held deep social meaning.

1980s. FM radio and the music video expanded popular music's reach, exposing listeners to a variety of genres. Songs were more about having fun and some of the lighter aspects of life. Country music, meanwhile, experienced a comeback that produced a crossover effect in popular music. Songs, of course, were generally about relationships and lost love.

1990s. The early 1990s saw the advent of grunge rock, a movement that returned popular music to its folk roots. The song lyrics, however, focused on despair and social inequality. The influence of rap and hip-hop music spread, exposing America to the despair of urban youth.

21st century. While the music industry continued to rely on dance and hip-hop music to appeal to its youngest listeners, groups from as far back as the 1960s were making comebacks with hopeful messages—much like decades before. Country music, with its appeal to conservative American values, is grabbing a fair share of the audience.

For more information on how music helped shape eras of American history, see the *Music and Bugling* merit badge pamphlet.

Extra! Extra!

A *current event* is a topic that is covered in the news right now. It could be an election, an environmental issue, or a war. It could be a study that compares, for example, the grades of students from different ethnic groups, which prompts change in the education system. It also could be a trend; perhaps inflated prices are easing up or the stock market is enjoying an upward trend.

Current events do not just happen. They are the results of many events affecting each other. When you read about a current event, you should think about what caused the event and how it affects not just the people involved, but you as well.

For instance, maybe a tornado has blown through the Midwest, causing millions of dollars worth of damage to buildings and farms. Of course, a tornado itself is not caused by anything but nature. But why was there so much damage? Did the building codes go back to the Civil War era and were therefore outdated? Had the area been a farming community since Colonial times? If so, what will the farmers do now? And how does this affect you? Will your town now take another look at its building codes?

Time Lines

One way to help you understand about the historical causes of an event is to make a time line. A time line can show you how one event caused another event that caused another event, and so on.

For instance, President Kennedy's vision of putting a man on the moon didn't happen overnight, nor did it stop there. Many events over several decades set the action in motion, leading up to today, when scientists can place a robot on Mars to send pictures back to Earth.

Space Race: A Time Line

1957. The Soviet Union launches Sputnik I, the first Earth-orbiting satellite. A year later, the United States countered, launching a satellite of its own.

1958. The United States forms the National Aeronautics and Space Administration—the federal agency dedicated to exploring space.

1961. Both the United States and Russia send a man into space for the first time. In 1963, Russian Valentina Tereshkova becomes the first woman in space.

1965. Ed White becomes the first American to walk in space.

1968. The United States launches the first manned mission that orbits the moon.

1969. U.S. astronauts Neil Armstrong and Buzz Aldrin land the Apollo 11 lunar module on the surface of the moon.

1973. The United States employs rocket technology to launch Skylab, its first space station.

1975. American astronauts and Russian cosmonauts rendezvous in space and dock their ships together to complete joint experiments.

1981. The United States opens a new era in space flight with the launch of the first space shuttle.

1986. The first phase of the Mir space station is launched into Earth's orbit.

1990. The Hubble Space Telescope is launched.

1997. The Mars Pathfinder probe lands on the surface of Mars and sends back images of the planet's surface.

2001. The Near Earth Asteroid Rendezvous (NEAR) spacecraft lands on the surface of the asteroid Eros.

2003–2004. More Martian probes land on Mars and survey the planet.

Where to Find Current Events

Current events are easy to find. Read newspapers and newsmagazines, watch television news programs, and listen to radio news shows to find out what stories people think are important. You will find that newspapers and newsmagazines often provide more information, details, and background about a current event. Because they have the space to provide more information, newspapers and magazines are often the best sources for detailed current events. TV is great for finding out what is going on, but most of the time, local news programs have only a few minutes to report a story.

Fair and Balanced

Sometimes news stories will present the facts in a way that reflects the reporter's opinion. This is called *bias* and usually is not intentional, but you should watch for certain signs that a news report may not be as balanced as it could be.

Headlines. Headlines can be misleading or express an opinion. The sports headline "Titans Clobbered" basically means the same thing as "Titans Put Up Good Fight," that the Titans lost a game. But the first headline puts the Titans in a more negative light than the second.

Word choices. A report says that a controversial speaker is interrupted by "loud audience outbursts," when it also could have said "a handful of protestors." Do you think the reporter wants to show that people really objected to the speaker, or that objections are not important?

Placement. Is the story on the front page or way in the back? Where the editor has placed the story reflects how important he or she feels the story is.

Sources. Does the reporter talk to an equal number of experts on both sides of the story? Or is there just one opinion from one side of the issue versus three opinions from the other side? That can be a sign that the reporter feels a certain way about the story.

Titles. How does the reporter refer to the person he or she is interviewing? Calling someone a "militant activist" has a different tone than a "person who disagrees with the government."

With your parent's permission, search the World Wide Web for more information about current events.

Careers in American Heritage

The great thing about careers in American heritage is that there is a position out there for just about anyone. Employers are looking for people who can think independently, communicate well, have good research skills, and analyze situations to relate them to the task at hand. Studying American heritage gives you these skills and makes you a sought-after candidate.

Most people who want to work in American heritage major in history in college. Some positions require a master's or doctorate degree, especially if you want to teach. You also might consider being a museum curator, national park ranger, historic preservation officer, or archivist. These fields require knowledge of a specific part of history.

Other fields may not relate directly to history but to skills learned while studying.

- Many lawyers have an undergraduate degree in history because knowledge of history is necessary to understand America's legal system.

- Journalists must be able to translate what someone has said or done into something the rest of us can understand. They also need to be able to find information, which requires research skills. You learn both these skills while studying history.

- The federal, state, and local governments often look for employees who do not have a particular specialty. They want people who can think critically, communicate, and understand how the American government works. Learning about history gives you those skills.

The American Dream

You have read about the contributions of many people, from the colonists to your peers of today. People immigrate to the United States from all over the globe for religious freedom, equal opportunity, education, and economic prosperity, among many of the freedoms some of us might take for granted.

Immigrants from around the world have heard the promise of the American dream and come here to pursue it. The term "American dream" was first used by James Truslow Adams in his 1931 book *The Epic of America.* Adams defines the American dream as "a land in which life should be better and richer and fuller for everyone, with opportunity for each according to ability or achievement." The American dream includes all those things we hold dear, from going to the movies to hearing the cheers of a high school football game to reading the Sunday comics.

What is it that makes America so attractive? Being American means that we can make many choices. We can choose where we live, what we do for a living, how we entertain ourselves, and even when we want a turkey sandwich for lunch. Not all peoples of the world have the freedom to make such choices.

The offer of freedom to the world's people is enticing. Our freedom began as a vision in the minds and hearts of the colonists, and it has flourished. Every generation of Americans has fought to protect that freedom against those who have tried to take it away—in world wars, cold wars, and wars on terrorism. Our heritage is how we as Americans got here, and understanding our ancestors' actions of yesterday is the first step to continuing the dream for generations to come.

James Truslow Adams theorizes that anyone in our culture can rise to great heights, depending on how much work he or she is willing to put into it.

The American Dreamers

American dreamers come from all walks of life, and they all have something special to share about why they hold this country and American heritage so dear. The following excerpts come from the Academy of Achievement, a nonprofit organization that is "dedicated to the education and inspiration of youth" through its Museum of the American Dream, which features "leaders who have shaped the modern world." Visit the Academy's Web site at *http://www.achievement.org* to learn more about these extraordinary individuals.

"The American Dream to me means that you have the ability to determine where you're going. You have the ability to formulate your dream, and you have the ability to put in motion all the building blocks that will help you achieve it. And I am so grateful that I was born in America."
—Benjamin Carson, M.D., pediatric neurosurgeon

"This is a nation whose spoken and written vision is chillingly beautiful. That each should have an opportunity. That work will get you where you need to be. That we need to respect each other, including our differences. That's a mighty vision; it's a precious way to talk about the American democracy."
—Johnnetta B. Cole, Ph.D., past president, Spelman College

"I have just an absolutely unshakeable belief about the value of living in freedom, that people who live in freedom . . . prevail over people who live in oppression. . . . Once you give people freedom, they don't willingly give it up."
—Rudolph Giuliani, former mayor of New York City

"In other countries, when you try and fail, you really fail. People really basically look at you as a failure. Here, people look at that as an excellent experience. . . . Only in the United States, people take that kind of attitude that we all need to take a risk. If it doesn't work out, at least I was brave enough that I did try it."
—Jeong H. Kim, Ph.D., entrepreneur from Korea

"The American Dream . . . represents a responsibility to share it, and to not just sort of hoard that freedom, but hopefully share that freedom with other countries."
—Maya Lin, designer of the Vietnam Veterans Memorial

American Heritage Resources

Scouting Literature

American Business, American Cultures, American Labor, Citizenship in the Community, Citizenship in the Nation, Citizenship in the World, Genealogy, Journalism, and *Law* merit badge pamphlets

Visit the Boy Scouts of America's official retail Web site (with your parent's permission) at *http://www.scoutstuff.org* for a complete listing of all merit badge pamphlets and other helpful Scouting materials and supplies.

Books

Bjornlund, Lydia. *The U.S. Constitution: Blueprint for Democracy.* Lucent Books Inc., 1999.

Carnes, Mark, ed. *Past Imperfect: History According to the Movies.* Holt and Company, 1995.

Dickson, Paul. *Timelines: Day by Day and Trend by Trend From the Dawn of the Atomic Age to the Gulf War.* Addison-Wesley Publishing, 1991.

Faber, Doris, and Harold Faber. *We the People: The Story of the United States Constitution Since 1787.* Charles Scribner's Sons, 1987.

Finlayson, Reggie, ed. *We Shall Overcome: The History of the American Civil Rights Movement.* Lerner Publishing Group, 2002.

Freedman, Russell. *Give Me Liberty! The Story of the Declaration of Independence.* Holiday House, 2000.

Hoose, Phillip M. *We Were There, Too!: Young People in U.S. History.* Farrar, Straus, and Giroux, 2001.

Jaffe, Steven H. *Who Were the Founding Fathers? Two Hundred Years of Reinventing American History.* Henry Holt and Co., 1996.

Kassinger, Ruth. *U.S. Census: A Mirror of America.* Raintree Steck-Vaughn Publishers, 2000.

McIntire, Suzanne. *American Heritage Book of Great American Speeches for Young People.* Sagebrush, 2001.

Torricelli, Robert, and Andrew Carroll, eds. *In Our Own Words: Extraordinary Speeches of the American Century.* Kodan-Sha International, 1999.

Wilson, Richard Guy, ed. *A Guide to Popular U.S. Landmarks as Listed in the National Register of Historic Places.* Franklin Watts Inc., 2003.

Zeinert, Karen. *Free Speech: From Newspapers to Music Lyrics.* Enslow Publishers, 1995.

Periodicals

American Heritage
Telephone: 212-367-3100
Web site: *http://www.americanheritage.com/magazine*

American History and Civil War Times
Telephone: 703-771-9400

Early American Life
Telephone: 440-543-8566
Web site: *http://www.ealonline.com*

Preservation
Telephone: 202-588-6388
Web site: *http://www.nationaltrust.org/magazine*

Organizations and Web Sites

Academy of Achievement
Telephone: 202-887-0000
Web site: *http://www.achievement.org*

America Singing: 19th Century Song Sheets
Web site: *http://memory.loc.gov/ammem/amsshtml/amsshome.html*

America's Library
Web site:
http://www.americaslibrary.gov

The American Family Immigration History Center
Telephone: 212-561-4588
Web site: *http://www.ellisisland.org*

American Veterans (AMVETS)
Toll-free telephone: 877-726-8387
Web site: *http://www.amvets.org*

Family Search Internet Genealogy Service
Web site: *http://www.familysearch.org*

Federal Depository Library Program
Web site: *http://www.gpoaccess.gov/libraries.html*

Genealogy.com
Web site: *http://www.genealogy.com*

TheHistoryNet: Where History Lives on the Web
Telephone: 703-771-9400
Web site: *http://www.historynet.com*

The Lester S. Levy Collection of Sheet Music
Johns Hopkins University
Web site:
http://levysheetmusic.mse.jhu.edu

Library of Congress
Telephone: 202-707-5000
Web site: *http://www.loc.gov*

National Constitution Center
Telephone: 215-409-6600
Web site:
http://www.constitutioncenter.org

National Park Service
Telephone: 202-208-6843
Web site: *http://www.nps.gov*

National Register of Historic Places
Telephone: 202-354-2213
Web site: *http://www.cr.nps.gov/nr/listing.htm*

Smithsonian Institution
Telephone: 202-633-1000
Web site: *http://www.si.edu*

U.S. Census Bureau
Telephone: 301-763-4636
Web site: *http://www.census.gov*

U.S. Government Printing Office
Telephone: 202-512-0000
Web site: *http://www.gpoaccess.gov*

The White House
Telephone: 202-456-1414
Web site: *http://www.whitehouse.gov*

Veterans of Foreign Wars (VFW)
Web site: *http://www.vfw.org*

Acknowledgments

The Boy Scouts of America thanks Darryl Hamson for his time, assistance, and expertise in updating this edition of the *American Heritage* merit badge pamphlet. Mr. Hamson is a costumed interpreter at Colonial Williamsburg in Williamsburg, Virginia, the largest living history museum in America.

The BSA is grateful to the American Library Association for its assistance with the resources section of this pamphlet. The ALA has a special committee that very effectively serves the merit badge pamphlet series in this capacity.

Photo and Illustration Credits

America's Library, courtesy— pages 8 *(top)*, 18, 34–35 *(both)*, and 38 *(bottom)*

Stephen Hernandez, courtesy— page 53 *(both)*

Historical-flag.com, courtesy— page 14 *(top)*

Historyimages.com, courtesy—page 10

JFK Library, courtesy—page 53

©Jupiterimages.com—cover *(all except merit badge, Colonist)*; pages 6, 14 *(bottom)*, 16 *(top)*, 17 *(top)*, 19, 39, 44 *(top)*, and 47 *(top)*

Krause Publications, Iola, Wisconsin, and Stack's Rare Coins, New York, New York, courtesy— page 16 *(bottom)*

Library of Congress Prints and Photographs Division, courtesy— pages 13, 17 *(bottom)*, 21, 24, 28 *(bottom)*, 38 *(top)*, 41, and 48

NASA, courtesy—pages 27 and 56 *(all)*

National Archives and Records Administration, courtesy—pages 8 *(bottom)* and 26

National Park Service, Frederick Douglass National Historic Site, courtesy—page 37

©Photos.com—pages 30 *(background)* and 59

Wikipedia.org, courtesy—pages 11 *(both)*, 25, and 44 *(bottom)*

Wikipedia.org/Harald Klinke, courtesy—page 47 *(bottom)*

Wikipedia.org/Dan Smith, courtesy— page 28 *(top)*

All other photos and illustrations not mentioned above are the property of or are protected by the Boy Scouts of America.

David Burke—page 23

Tom Copeland Jr.—cover *(Colonist)*; pages 4, 9, 12, 42, 45, and 46 *(bottom)*

Roy Jansen—page 36

Randy Piland—pages 30 *(foreground)* and 57

Notes